HOW TO FALL MADLY IN LOVE WITH YOURSELF AND YOUR BODY

DANIELLE SWABY

To my Mom who took me to the gym when I was in my worst shape in all aspects, it changed my life. Thank you!

LOVE QUESTIONNAIRE
Answer YES, NO, or NOT SURE for each question:

1. Do you know what real love is?
2. Would you speak to others the way you speak to yourself?
3. When you look in the mirror do you love what you see?
4. Have you forgiven yourself and others for past regrets?
5. Are you free from comparing yourself to others?
6. Do you treat your body the best you can?
7. Do you have a definite purpose for your life?

If you answered no to even one of these questions you may be holding yourself back from truly loving yourself and your body. Over the next thirty-one days we will uncover and remove what is blocking you from falling madly in love with yourself and your body.

How to use this book:

1. Read one chapter per day, preferably first thing in the morning.
2. Do the exercises provided, there is an exercise for your mind and body.
3. Memorize and meditate on the verse provided, meditate just means to think on it.
4. There are lined pages available for you to journal and look back on your progress in the future!
5. Enjoy the process.

Introduction

I commend you for taking action towards loving yourself and your body more deeply. I already know that you are amazing, strong, and lovable. It's your turn to know it.

I wrote this book originally as a journal for myself. I began keeping journals when I was seven years old. Reading them now they crack me up and just as easily can bring tears to my eyes. I've been the little girl that wondered why I had such frizzy hair, when all I wanted was shiny smooth hair. I was the teenager who decided it was worth it not to eat so that I could be skinny. I've been the young woman that thought hooking up means he likes you. I've been the insecure woman who filled her own mind with can't and not good enough. I've been where so many girls and woman have been and where many still are.

Through writing and doing the exercises in this book I began to feel more love in every area of my life. I felt a pull on my heart to share this because I know I am not alone in how I have felt.

This is dedicated to girls and women at every and any age. You deserve to feel amazing in your body and you deserve to love yourself and your life every day.

The time to start is right now.

With love,

Danielle Swaby

DAY 1

What is love?

"Love endures long and is patient and kind, love never is envious nor boils over with jealousy, is not boastful or vainglorious, does not display itself haughtily. It is not conceited; it is not rude and does not act unbecomingly. Love does not insist on its own rights or its own way, for it is not self-seeking; it is not touchy or fretful or resentful; it takes no account of the evil done to it. It pays no attention to a suffered wrong. It does not rejoice at injustice and unrighteousness, but rejoices when right and truth prevail. Love bears up under anything and everything that comes, and is ever ready to believe the best of every person, its hopes are fadeless under all circumstances, and it endures everything (without weakening). Love never fails.
1 Corinthians 13: 4-8

I'm sure you've heard the above verse before, maybe at a wedding or special occasion. Do you believe this definition of love? In order to have something you must first understand what it is that you want. Because you are reading this book I am going to assume you are ready to fall madly in love with yourself and your body. So now that you know what love is we are going to begin with you. To love ourselves we must be patient, kind, and forgiving to ourselves. Before we can ever attempt to love another, we must fully understand we cannot give away what we do not have. Today we will begin by loving ourselves truly and deeply with full understanding of what love is. I suggest reading over the above verse and perhaps writing it, memorizing it, and meditating on it today. To understand what love is and to begin loving yourself is the first step in loving your body! Your body begins where it is today. This body has carried you through life thus far. Whether it is broken, bruised or tired it is yours and you will not be getting another. It is time to appreciate how far this body has taken you and decide to commit to it and love it exactly as it is today. You will now take care of your body and treat it with respect and love. It is all uphill from here. The decisions that you make after today will reflect the new love you have for yourself and your body.

"You've been criticizing yourself for years and it hasn't worked. Try approving of yourself and see what happens."
Louise L. Hay

Exercise

Love: List 7 things you love about yourself:

1. _____
2. _____
3. _____
4. _____
5. _____
6. _____
7. _____

Body: List 7 amazing things your body has done:

1. _____
2. _____
3. _____
4. _____
5. _____
6. _____
7. _____

Memorize and meditate:
You are altogether beautiful my love there is no flaw in you.
Song of Solomon 4:7

DAY 2

God is Love.

Beloved, let us love one another, for love is from God; and he who loves is begotten (born) of God and is coming to know and understand God. He who does not love has not become acquainted with God, for God is love.
1 John 4:7-8

We were made to love, to be loved, to be loving, to love one another and to love ourselves! God made us exactly as he wanted us. Each one of us is detailed as he planned. God loves us just as we are today. He only has good planned for you. He wants the best for you. Know that God is good.

Exercise
Love: List 7 things you are grateful for today.

1. _____
2. _____
3. _____
4. _____
5. _____
6. _____
7. _____

Body: List 7 beautiful features of your body.

1. _____
2. _____
3. _____
4. _____
5. _____
6. _____
7. _____

Memorize and Meditate:
For you formed my inward parts; you knitted me together in my Mother's womb. I praise you, Lord I am fearfully and wonderfully made.
Psalm 139:13 – 14

DAY 3

Find Peace

Now the mind of the flesh is death. But the mind of the spirit is life and peace.
Romans 8:6

When you feel anxious or uneasy this is not a feeling from God. When God is speaking to you he leaves you with a feeling of peace, joy, and ease. Follow your peaceful feelings and steer away from things that take away your peace.

Exercise
Love: Name three things that bring you the most peace.
    1. _____
    2. _____
    3. _____

How can you do more of these things?

_____
_____
_____

Body: What three physical activities do you enjoy the most?
    1. _____
    2. _____
    3. _____

Choose one of the above to do as your exercise today.

Memorize and meditate:
Be anxious for nothing but in everything by prayer and supplication with thanksgiving let your requests be made known to God.
Philippians 4:6

DAY 4

Renew your mind

Strip yourselves of your former nature which characterized your previous manner of life and becomes corrupt through lusts and desires that spring from delusion; and be constantly renewed in the spirit of your mind having a fresh mental and spiritual attitude and put on the new nature created in God's image in true righteousness and holiness.
Ephesians 4:22-24

Your thoughts guide your life. Your thoughts are a magnet for what you attract into your life. If you are not enjoying the outcomes of your life you must begin by changing your thoughts.
"Think about what you've been thinking about."
-   **Joyce Meyer**

Do you speak to and about yourself kindly? Is your self-talk loving? Do you discourage yourself or compliment and motivate yourself? When you look in the mirror is it to find your flaws or embrace your unique beauty. Become aware. Today you begin to change your thoughts, words, and actions. Do not expect others to treat you better than you would treat yourself. You set the tone. You set the standard. This is a challenge, but it is necessary. You must become aware of your thoughts, and renew your mind in order to fall madly in love with yourself and your body.

Exercise

Love: Put on a new piece of jewelry, I love a ring, make this a promise to yourself and a reminder that you will talk to yourself in a loving way. As soon as you begin to think or say something mean to yourself look at that ring (or jewelry) and switch the thought and the words to something kind and loving.

Body: Look at yourself. What do you love? Name three unique beautiful things about your body.

1. _____

2. _____

3. _____

Memorize and meditate:

Let us strip off and throw aside every encumbrance (unnecessary weight) and the sin which so readily clings to and entangles us.

Hebrews 12:1

DAY 5

Be Patient

Let us run with patient endurance and steady and active persistence the appointed course of the race that is set before us.
Hebrews 12:1

We must be patient with ourselves. Part of being loving to others and ourselves is having patience. We are going to mess up, say the wrong things, make silly mistakes, eat what we are "not supposed to eat" and likely miss some days that we "should" be working out. Dwelling on what we should have done will not help the situation. Thinking about it repeatedly will only create anxiety and make you mad at yourself. Instead choose to learn from your actions and decide what you will do next time. Forgive yourself, let it go and move on! If we are not patient with ourselves it will feel overwhelming to be patient with others and unfair to ask others to be patient with us. The course is laid out in front of us. Focus on what must be done for you to achieve your goal now. Complete that. Embrace the action you took. Be proud and happy with each step you take. Tell yourself good job. You will not grow tired and impatient if you stay focused and embrace each action in the moment.

Exercise
Love: What have I been circling around in my mind that I regret?

_____

_____

_____Make a new decision about what you will do next time.

_____

_____

_____

Let it go.

Body: Have I been impatient with my body? In what way?

_____

_____

_____ What is one step I can take today to keep me on the path to my body goals?

_____

_____

_____

Memorize and meditate:
Be completely humble, gentle; be patient. Bearing with one another in love.
Ephesians 4:2

I therefore, the prisoner for the Lord, appeal to and beg you to walk worthy of the divine calling to which you have been called with complete lowliness of mind and meekness, with patience bearing one another and making allowances because you love one another. Be eager and strive earnestly to guard and keep the harmony and oneness of the spirit in the binding power of peace.
There is one body and one spirit just as there is also one hope that belongs to the calling you received.
Ephesians 4:1-4

DAY 6

Free Yourself

Look away from all that will distract to Jesus, Who is the leader and the source of our faith and is also its finisher. He, for the joy that was set before Him, endured the cross, despising and ignoring the shame, and is now seated at the right hand of the throne of God.
Hebrews 12:2

Look at your life. Is there anything holding you back from achieving the goals you have set for yourself? People? Activities? Thoughts? Habits? Friends? Really take inventory and decide to clean up your life where necessary. Let nothing hold you back from living as the best most lovable you.

EXERCISE
Love: What is stopping you from reaching your goals?

_____

_____

_____ What are you going
to do about it right now?

_____

_____

_____

Body: What is stopping you from reaching your body goals?

_____

_____

_____

What are you going to do about it right now?

_____

_____

_____

Memorize and Meditate:
Do you not know that in a race all the runners compete, but
only one receives the prize? So run your race that you may lay
hold of the prize and make it yours.
1 Corinthians 9:24

DAY 7

Have Faith

For as he thinks in his heart so is he.
Proverbs 23:7

Faith is complete trust or confidence in something or someone. What you choose to believe in your heart becomes your truth. Faith is something that can be strengthened. Just as you can learn to control your thoughts you can learn to strengthen your faith. You can choose what you will believe. Begin to believe that you are lovable. Your body is lovable. You and your body are lovable exactly as they are right now. Tell yourself you are lovable. Tell yourself your body is lovable. Repeat this daily, multiple times a day and all day! Your belief in love for yourself will begin to grow. It is up to no one but yourself to create the belief that you are able to be loved. You cannot wait for acceptance from others, because frankly it may never come. There are a lot of broken people in this world and if someone hasn't understood how to love themselves how can you trust the love that they plan to share with you? Have trust in yourself that you can love yourself deeply. God loves you. Exactly as you are. Your turn.

She opens her mouth in skillful and godly wisdom and on her tongue is the law of kindness.
Proverbs 31:26

Exercise

Love: God loves you. Say it 10 times. Believe it. Tell yourself "I love you" 10 times.

Body: Say it "I love my body" 10 times. What do you want from your body?

_____

_____

_____

What are you going to do to get what you want?

_____

_____

_____

You will have your body goals by:

_____

Why?

_____

_____

_____

The plan is set.

Memorize and meditate
Wait for it, because it will surely come; it will not be behindhand on its appointed day.
Habakkuk 2:3

DAY 8

Your Body

Do you not know that your body is the temple of the Holy Spirit who lives within? Whom you have received from God. You are not your own. You were bought with a price. So then honor God and bring glory to him in your body.
1 Corinthians 6:19-20

Your body is precious. It is God's creation. God created you and made you perfectly, exactly as he wanted you. Do not believe the standards that the world has set for beautiful and perfect, they are only based on opinion and most of the time a ridiculous opinion. Your body is God's handiwork, his masterpiece. When you accept Jesus into your heart, when you decide you want to do and be good your body becomes a holy place and the spirit of Jesus lives inside you. How would you treat a precious body? How would you treat the body of a newborn innocent baby? With tender kindness and respect I am sure! Let's get back to that. Remember the moment you lost your innocence. Remember the moment you began to feel less than perfect. It's time to let go of what happened in the past and bring back your innocence. Know that you are a daughter/son of the King. Treat your body like royalty. Royalty lives in you. You are worthy. Let the actions and behaviors of your body speak for you.

Exercise
Love: What actions must I remove from my life right now to bring respect to myself?

_____

_____

_____

Visualize the impression you would like to leave on people. Describe it.

_____

_____

_____

Body: What actions must I remove & add into my life right now to bring greater respect to my body?

_____

_____

_____

_____

Visualize your body in its best shape, best posture, most confident. What is your demeanor like? Describe yourself.

_____

_____

_____

Memorize and meditate:
Do you not discern and understand that you are God's temple? And that God's spirit has his permanent dwelling in you.
1Corinthians 3:16

If anyone does hurt to God's temple or corrupts or destroys it, God will do hurt to him and bring him to the corruption of death and destroy him. For the temple of God is holy and you are.
1 Corinthians 3:16-17

DAY 9

Love others

Love your neighbor as yourself.
Luke 10:27

You can only give what you have. To love others, we must first have love for ourselves. God commands us to love each other. That means he is commanding us to love ourselves. He is commanding us to love ourselves and everyone. Not only the people that are kind to us, everyone. You are always with yourself. Once the day is over you are alone and why shouldn't you enjoy it? You deserve to love yourself all day long! God loves you. He loves everything about you. Even things you find to be flaws. He loves them. Start enjoying yourself exactly as you are right now. Not when you lose 20lbs, get a husband, have the butt, arms, job, things, you desire. Start loving yourself now. As is. Exactly as you are. Make yourself capable of giving love to others by first loving yourself.

Love your enemies and pray for those who persecute you.
Matthew 5:44

For if you love those who love you, what reward can you have? Do not even the tax collectors do that? And if you greet only your brethren, what more than others are you doing? Do not even the Gentiles do that?
Matthew 5:46-47

To be a bigger person, a more loving person we need to treat people differently. We need to love the people that seem unlovable. It is easy to love people that we like, the people that are "easy" to love but God wants us to love those that are more difficult to love. He wants us to love the broken, the wounded and the hurt souls. Think about someone who was kind to you when they had no need to be. That feeling that they left with you, don't you want to leave that with someone else? You can make a difference in someone's life, maybe even save a life by simply being kind.

Be not afraid, only believe.
Mark 5:36

Exercise
Love: Who can you pray for that hasn't been kind to you or perhaps even hurt you?

_____

_____

_____

How can you love them?

_____

_____

_____

Body: Do something kind for your body today. Go for a run then take a nice long shower, fix your nails, your hair, look your best even if it is just for you!
Set a new standard for yourself today.

Memorize and meditate:
She is more precious than jewels and her worth is far above rubies or pearls.
Proverbs 31:10

DAY 10

Ignite the effort

*By means of these He has bestowed on us his precious and exceedingly great promises, so that through them you may escape from the moral decay that is in the world because of covetousness (lust and greed) and become sharers of the divine nature. For this very reason, adding your diligence, employ every effort in exercising your faith to develop virtue, and in exercising virtue develop knowledge, and in exercising knowledge develop self-control, and in exercising self-control develop steadfastness, and in exercising steadfastness develop godliness, and in exercising godliness develop brotherly affection, and in exercising brotherly affection develop Christian love. For as these qualities are yours and increasingly abound in you, they will keep you from being idle or unfruitful unto the full, personal, knowledge of our Lord Jesus Christ the Messiah, the anointed one.
II Peter 1:4-8*

See how the verse above says to first develop and then it says exercise. To develop these qualities, you must try with strategic attempts to develop these seven qualities and once you develop these qualities you must exercise them. Just as you would train a muscle to make them stronger, you'll need to train these qualities in yourself. if you are not growing stronger you are growing weaker. Developing and exercising these qualities will make you a more whole, lovely, loving, lovable, likeable person.

Exercise

Love: Memorize the 7 qualities the Bible says to develop diligently.

1. Virtue
2. Knowledge
3. Self- control
4. Steadfastness
5. Godliness
6. Brotherly affection
7. Christian love

Body: what actions can you take for each of the above qualities?

1. Virtue

_____

2. Knowledge

_____

3. Self-control

_____

4. Steadfastness

_____

5. Godliness

_____

6. Brotherly Affection

_____

7. Christian Love

_____

Memorize and meditate:
Live purposefully and worthily and accurately not as the unwise and witless but as wise people making the most of the time.
Ephesians 5:1

DAY 11

Enjoy the process

Rejoice O young man in your adolescence, and let your heart cheer you in the days of your full-grown youth. And walk in the ways of your heart and in the sight of your eyes but know that for all these things God will bring you into judgement.
Ecclesiastes 4:9

Life is short. Enjoy it. Follow your heart's and your deepest desires. Let God's peace be your guide. The things you do matter. Live purposefully, joyfully, and in a way that pleases God and you will be blessed!

Exercise
Love: What do you enjoy most in life?

_____

_____

_____

Body: When does your body feel the best?

_____

_____

_____

Memorize and meditate
O taste and see that the Lord our God is good! Blessed is
the man who trusts and takes refuge in him.
Psalm 34:8

DAY 12

Be strong

Have I not commanded you? Be strong, vigorous and very courageous. Do not be afraid. I am the Lord your God. I am with you wherever you go. Joshua 1:9

Strength is the emotional or mental qualities necessary for events that are distressing or difficult. Life is not always going to be a piece of cake. You will need strength to get through life without being frazzled or broken down by disappointments. It may not be easy but it is totally possible. Commit to the person you intend to be. Commit to the vision you have for yourself and DO NOT GIVE UP!
"Everything you ever wanted is on the other side of fear!"
Jack Canfield
When you follow your heart and your peace amazing things can happen. This life is short. There is a time for everything. Live your life with a vision and with a purpose. Live courageously and fearlessly. YOU CAN DO IT.

True wisdom is a strength to the wise man more than ten rulers or valiant generals who are in the city. Ecclesiastes 7:19

Exercise

Love: Has there been something on your heart to do, but you've been too afraid? Take a step today. Do it.

Body: Strengthen your body today in a new way. Lift weights, do yoga do something different.

Memorize and meditate:
He has made everything beautiful in its time.
Ecclesiastes 3:11

DAY 13

Focus on God

You will guard him and keep him in perfect and constant peace whose mind (both its inclination and its character) is stayed on You, because he commits himself to You, leans on You, and hopes confidently in You.
So trust in the Lord (commit yourself to Him, lean on Him and hope confidently in Him) forever; for the Lord God is an everlasting Rock.
Isaiah 26: 3- 4

There is a spiritual warfare going on, the battle of good and evil. The closer we get to God and his holiness we will be challenged. The enemy seeks to destroy. The enemy wants you lose your peace, he will use others to test you. God will also test you to make sure you are ready to handle more opportunities. People will test you when they see you doing well. Sometimes they want to see you fail. That is fine. You are armored with the strength of God. He is your rock. Your power and salvation. You are planted with a strong foundation you will not fall if you keep your focus and trust on him. He's got your back.

Exercise

Love: Take time today to speak with God and ask him to help you focus on him in times of testing, challenges, and temptation. *Consider each test to be an opportunity to upgrade yourself to allow him to build your strength and character.*

Body: Let your body be challenged. Get uncomfortable. Do the uncomfortable again. Feel sore in new places. Get stronger.

Memorize and meditate:
She laughs without fear of the future.
Proverbs 31:25

DAY 14

Obey

For I know the thoughts and plans that I have for you, says the Lord, thoughts and plans for welfare and peace and not for evil, to give you hope in your final outcome.
Jeremiah 29:11

God has a great plan for your life. He is working on your problems as you continue living each day. He already knew the days of your life before you lived them. Trust him and obey him. God's plan is better than you can ever imagine. How do you obey God? He is in you – he is your peace -your conscience will tell you if something is from him or not from God. Listen to your conscience, follow your peace. You do not always need the opinions and advice of others. All the advice you need is already in you. There are times to seek counsel, and there are times it is not necessary, instead wait for God, listen to what he gives you peace about and obey that.

Exercise:
Love: Is there an area of your life God has been speaking to you about? Maybe something he would like you to stop doing? Obey.
Body: Are you obeying God in how you are handling your body? Sexually and In a healthy way? Are you taking the best care of you, you can?
Obey what is on your heart.

Memorize and meditate:
Delight yourself also in the Lord and he will give you the desires and secret petitions of your heart.
Psalm 37:4

DAY 15

Pass your tests

For the rest brethren, whatever is true, whatever is worthy of reverence and is honorable and seemly whatever is just, whatever is pure, whatever is lovely and lovable, whatever is kind and winsome and gracious, if there is any virtue and excellence, if there is anything worthy of praise, think on and weigh and take account of these things! Practice what you have learned and received and heard and seen in me, and model your way of living on it, and The God of peace will be with you.
Philippians 4:8-9

You will be tested. By people, by circumstances, by situations, and disappointments. Your peace will be challenged. In these moments remember God's plan is better than you can ever imagine. Whatever is happening in this moment – even if it is unpleasant is part of God's plan. His plan is good. He may be removing people from your life or clearing out opportunities because he has something better! Think about the good things. Keep your mind focused on your goals. Stay positive. Find the good, the blessing and the opportunity in every situation. At times the devil will try to shake you and break you. Pass the test! Do not get shaken or broken. Other times God is testing you to see if he can move you to even greater positions.

Exercise:
Love: Have you been challenged lately? By who? Did you pass?

_____

_____

_____

_____

Body: What has been your greatest challenge and distraction to your body goals? What can you do today to overcome?

_____

_____

_____

_____

Memorize and meditate:
Those who wait for the Lord shall change and renew their strength and power; they shall lift their wings and mount up as eagles they shall run and not be weary they shall walk and not faint or become tired.
Isaiah 40:31

DAY 16

Rest

He rested on the seventh day from all his work which he had done. And God blessed the seventh day, set it apart as His own, and hallowed it, because on it God rested from all His work which He had created and done.
Genesis 2:2-3

Rest. Review all the work you have done on yourself so far. Review the results you have gained. The body, the soul, and the heart all needs rest. Relax in the peace of knowing that everything your working on is coming. Trust that God is good and while you rest God continues to make things happen for your good. Rest and recovery are important for the body to repair and grow stronger. The same concept goes for the mind. Enjoy your rest today.

Exercise:
RELAX

Memorize and meditate:
Come to me all you who labor and are heavy laden and
overburdened and I will cause you to rest.
Matthew 11:28

Take my yoke upon you and learn of me, for I am gentle and humble in heart and you will find rest (relief and ease and refreshment and recreation and blessed quiet) for your souls. For my yoke is wholesome (useful, good – not harsh, hard, sharp or pressing, but comfortable, gracious and pleasant) and my burden is light and easy to be borne.
Matthew 11:29-30

DAY 17

Simplify

And the Lord answered me and said, write the vision and engrave it so plainly upon tablets that everyone who passes may read easily as he hastens by. For the vision is yet for an appointed time and it hastens to the end; it will not deceive or disappoint. Though it tarry, wait earnestly for it, because it will surely come; it will not be behindhand on its appointed day. Look at the proud, his soul is not straight or right within him but the just and the uncompromisingly righteous man shall live by his faith and in his faithfulness. Habakkuk 2:2-4

You know what has been on your heart for a while now. You know what you must do. Keep it simple. Complete the tasks at hand. Focus on the vision. If you need your vision to become clearer ask God to give you a vision. **And whatever you ask for in prayer, having faith and really believing, you will receive. Matthew 21:22** Do not give up because the timing isn't what you planned it is not on your timing – it's God's timing and he knows what is best – there are other factors and circumstances God may be waiting on for you. Keep it simple do the little things daily that you must do to see the big results later.

Exercise
Love: What projects or tasks have been on your heart to complete?

_____

_____

_____

Do it. You will feel more accomplished, peaceful, proud and loving towards yourself for doing so.

Body: What daily tasks must you do to accomplish your body goals?

_____

_____

_____Do it. It's your turn to get everything you ever wanted.

Memorize and meditate:
For he is not a God of confusion and disorder but of peace and order.
1 Corinthians 14:33

DAY 18

Wait

For we through the Holy Spirit's help, by faith anticipate and wait for the blessing and good for which our righteousness and right standing with God, to hope (our conformity to His will in purpose, thought and action) causes us to hope. Galatians 5:5

God's timing is perfect. Be still. Wait. Listen to the peace in your heart. No understanding or explanation is necessary. He knows what he is doing. Practice patience. Practice faith. Practice trust. Be still in knowing you are on the right track. Stay steady.

Exercise:
Love: Where can you be more patient?

_____

_____

_____

Body: Are you trusting and enjoying the process? Can you try harder?

_____

_____

_____

Memorize and meditate:
Lean on, trust in, and be confident in the Lord with all your heart and mind and do not rely on your own insight or understanding.
Proverbs 3:5

DAY 19

Consistency

Blessed is the man who is patient under trial and stands up under temptation, for when he has stood the test and been approved, he will receive the victor's crown of life which God has promised to those who love him.
James 1:12

Stay stable, consistent, strong. If you reach bumps in the road and "mess up" or get distracted do not let this defeat you!

"Do not take defeat seriously."
Napoleon Hill

Trials will come. Pass them they are all tests. Temptation will come, defeat it, it is only a test. They may come in forms of people, circumstances, disappointments, or setbacks.
Stay consistent with the steps you must take daily. There is a reward waiting for you!

Exercise
Love: Where can you practice more consistency in your relations with yourself and others?

_____

_____

_____

Body: Have you hit a delay in progress because of a missed workout, a binge, being sick, a life change or a distraction? Today is the day to recharge and take charge! Prepare your meals, get your workout in. Do what you need to do. DO NOT GIVE UP.
List three habits you declare to do consistently starting today to reach your body goals:
    1. _____
    2. _____
    3. _____

Memorize and meditate:
She is clothed in strength and dignity and she laughs without fear of the future.
Proverbs 31:25

DAY 20

God is Good

O taste and see that the Lord (our God) is good!
Blessed is the man who trusts and takes refuge in him.
Psalm 34:8

God is good! He wants the best for you and I in every way.
For us to enjoy life, love each other, be loved, laugh, and feel
amazing. Delight yourself today in all that God has already
done in your life. Count your blessings and rejoice.

Exercise

Love: What amazing things has God done in your life? List 7 things from day 1!

1. _____
2. _____
3. _____
4. _____
5. _____
6. _____
7. _____

Body: What changes have you seen in your attitude towards your body since day 1?

1. _____
2. _____
3. _____
4. _____
5. _____
6. _____
7. _____

Memorize and meditate:
Be still and rest in the Lord; Wait for him and patiently lean yourself upon him.
Psalm 37:7

DAY 21

Believe

And whatever you ask for in prayer, having faith and really believing, you will receive.
Matthew 21:22

Ask. Believe. Receive.

Remove the clutter from your mind. Ask God out loud for what you need and desire. Believe he is almighty Lord and can fulfill your request. Receive it! Allow him to give you the desires of your heart and life he has planned for you!

Exercise
Love: What would you like to ask God for? Do it.

_____

_____

_____

Believe you will receive it, wait patiently and be ready to receive it.

Body: What would you like to ask for regarding your body and health?

_____

_____

_____

Ask. Believe. Receive.

Memorize and meditate:
Keep on asking and it will be given you; keep on seeking and you will find; keep on knocking and the door will be opened to you.
Matthew 7:7

DAY 22

Trust

May the God of your hope so fill you with all joy and peace in believing through the experience of your faith that by the power of the Holy Spirit you may abound and be overflowing with hope.
Romans 15:13

Have faith in the plan God has for your life. Believe that God has always had a plan for you and that despite any surprise twists and turns in your life the plan remains the same as its always been. God's plan has never changed for you. Consider everything to be part of it. Consider even the trials to be tests to renew your faith. Let yourself be overjoyed with happiness, excitement, and peace. You are on the right path, stay steady and stay excited! It's happening!

Exercise

Love: Listen to "Oceans" by Hillsong United

Spirit lead me where my trust is without borders. Let me walk upon the water wherever you would call me. Take me deeper than my feet could ever wander. And my faith will be made stronger in the presence of my savior.

Body: Stay consistent. When you work out, sweat. You are in the process. This is your story. This is your journey to your dream body. This is your dream body. Soon your story will inspire someone else.

Memorize and meditate:

Your eyes saw my unformed substance, and in your book all the days of my life were written before ever they took shape, when as yet there were none of them.

Psalm 139:16

DAY 23

A new thing

Behold, I am doing a new thing! Now it springs forth; do you not perceive and know it and will you not give heed to it? I will even make a way in the wilderness and rivers in the desert.
Isaiah 43:19

Let go and let God! Let go of the plans you had in your mind, let go of the past, let go of the upsets and unforgiveness you have in your heart. Let it all go. God can do a new thing at any time and it will be better than the old thing. Sometimes we have every detail of our lives planned that we don't even realize there are things that could be better for us. We don't know what we don't know. Let go and keep your eyes on eternal life with Jesus. Focus on being good and doing good, being kind, loving, having self-control and gaining knowledge. A great body can only get you so far but a great heart will give you eternal life.

Exercise
Love: What plans can I let go of and make room for God to work in my life?

_____

_____

_____

_____

Body: What ideas about what my body "should" look like can I let go of and release the pressure I put on myself?

_____

_____

_____

_____

Memorize and meditate:
Looking away from all that will distract to Jesus, who is the leader and the source of our faith.
Isaiah 12:2

DAY 24

Wisdom

For the word that God speaks is alive and full of power (making it active, operative, energizing and effective) It is sharper than any two -edged sword, penetrating to the dividing line of the breath of life (soul) and the immortal spirit and of joints and marrow (of the deepest parts of our nature) exposing and sifting and analyzing and judging the very thoughts and purposes of the heart.
Hebrews 4:12

Ask God for wisdom. Having a wise mind and an understanding heart is more valuable than any possessions you can obtain. God will give you what you ask for. He will be pleased with this request. The word of God is powerful and life changing. It exposes exactly who you are and the condition of your heart. Continue to study the word, allow God to make you who he intended you to be. It is more wonderful than you can imagine. Allow him to grow you and complete you for your purpose in this short life.

Exercise
Love: Ask God to make you wise.

So give your servant an understanding mind and a hearing heart to judge your people, that I may discern between good and bad. For who is able to judge and rule this your great people?
1 Kings 3:9

Body: Be wise in taking care of your body. Remember you want what is best for your body in the long run – good sleep – water – healthy foods – exercise. Find balance today.

Memorize and meditate:
Skillful and Godly wisdom is more precious than rubies; and nothing you can wish for is to be compared to her.
Proverbs 3:15

Day 25

Be Stronger

So those who are now last will be first then, and those who are first will be last then.
Matthew 20:16

You have a purpose everyone does, whether you follow through is up to you. It will not be easy. You will have to ignite your effort 100%. You will have to eliminate distractions daily. You will have to form good habits and follow through every day whether you are sick, tired, or heart broken. Your desire will need to be stronger that your willingness to quit. It will take everything in you. You will lose friends, family may scatter, people will disappear. You may not seem fun, or normal. But the reward will be everlasting and so fulfilling. You are doing it for a higher purpose beyond yourself. The best you for you is the best you for everyone. You are doing it for God.

Exercise
Love: Be stronger than your tests today, that means exercise your patience and kindness with people. Be love. Do not get frazzled. You are called. You are chosen.

Body: Do it. You know what you must do to stay on track with your body goals today. Do not delay. Do it.

Memorize and meditate:
Be strong vigorous and very courageous. Do not be afraid, I am the Lord your God, I am with you wherever you go. Joshua 1:9

DAY 26

Heal

But one thing I do (it is my one aspiration): forgetting what lies behind and straining forward to what lies ahead.
Philippians 3:13

It is time to heal. To completely let go of what was and what has been. To leave the past behind and move into the future. Ask God to relieve you and to heal your heart and soul and to give you a new vision for your future.
You are free!
You do not need to be defined by your past any more. You are new. You have been forgiven. You have learned right from wrong. Don't be upset with yourself for what you didn't know. It's over. It's done. Today is the day to set yourself free from all that happened previously. Let it all go! Great things are happening. Get excited. Choose to heal, to be healed, in the process of healing.

Exercise
Love: What definition of yourself can you let go of today?

_____

_____

_____

Define the new you!

_____

_____

_____

Body: What description of your old body will you let go of
today?

_____

_____Describe the new you!

_____

_____

_____

Memorize and meditate:
Beloved I pray that you may prosper in every way and that
your body may keep well even as I know your soul keeps well
and prospers.
III John 1:2

DAY 27

Finish

Better is the end of a thing than the beginning of it, and the patient in spirit is better than the proud in spirit.
Ecclesiastes 7:8

You are almost there. Stay steady and stay focused. Get done what you planned to get done. The reward will be worth it. Ignore distractions. Stay focused on the goal. You have been reading this to fall in love with yourself and your body. Do it. Finish.

Exercise
Love: What must I focus my mind on today to complete my task?

_____

_____ Body: What must I do today to ensure I complete my goal successfully?

_____

_____

_____

Memorize and meditate:
Do not therefore fling away your fearless confidence for it carries a great and glorious compensation of reward.
Hebrews 10:35

DAY 28

Pray boldly and have faith

If any of you is deficient in wisdom let him ask of the giving God who gives to everyone liberally and ungrudgingly, without reproaching or fault finding, and it will be given him.
James 1:5

Only it must be in faith that he asks with no wavering (no hesitating, no doubting) for the one who wavers Is like the billowing surge out at sea that is blown hither and thither and tossed by the wind.
James 1:6

Whatever it is you want ask God for it. Have faith that He is working on it and you will receive it at the exact and perfect time. There is no good or blessing in wanting and not asking. Remember? Ask, believe, receive! If it is not supposed to be yours you won't get it. Remember God's plan is perfect and it is already in the process. Effective prayer is done in faith. See what you want, see the details. Trust God.

Exercise
Love: What have you been wanting for yourself lately, in any regard (love, health, family, relationships, finance)?

_____

_____
_____ Ask.

Body: What do you need to get the body you truly desire at this point (confidence, motivation, energy, help)?

_____

_____

_____

Ask.

Memorize and meditate:
Let us fearlessly and confidently and boldly draw near to the throne of Grace that we may receive mercy and find grace to help in good time for every need.
Hebrews 4:16

DAY 29

Give thanks

Thank God in everything (no matter what the
circumstances may be, be thankful and give thanks)
for this is the will of God for you (who are) in Christ
Jesus (the revealer and mediator of that will).
1 Thessalonians 5:18

You have so much to be grateful for. Starting with the breath
you just took. This day. Your health. Your life. Each moment
leading to the next. This is all part of God's plan. Say thank
you. Appreciate. Like attracts like, meaning the more you are
grateful for, the more things to be grateful for will come into
your life. Even when circumstances are shaky remember
giving thanks is part of the plan. Something great is on the
way!

Exercise
Love: Count your blessings.

1. _____
2. _____
3. _____
4. _____
5. _____
6. _____
7. _____

Body: Count the blessings of your body. All the things it allows you to do!

1. _____
2. _____
3. _____
4. _____
5. _____
6. _____
7. _____

Memorize and meditate:
The Lord is my strength and my shield; my heart trusts in him and he helps me.
Psalm 28:7

DAY 30

Seek God 1st

But seek (aim at and strive after) first His kingdom and his righteousness (his ways of doing and being right) and then all these things taken together will be given you besides.
Matthew 6:33

Keep God first in your life. Strive to do and be good first and good things will come. It is easy to become distracted and begin to yearn and desire and lust after things that you start to believe will fulfill you. The only thing that will truly fulfill you is God. His love living in you will create happiness. Being loved by a relationship, friendships, having a perfect body, looking a certain way, will only fulfill you temporarily. This 31 day journey has been about falling madly in love with yourself and your body. The reality is you are falling in love with God and his wonderful creations, all of them, including YOU. Including other people! You are learning what love truly is. You are becoming love and living in love. Seek God first and seek love first and not only will love for yourself and your body be present and constant in your life. Love will fill your life in every way. I ask God to help you love more deeply and to fill your lives with an abundance of love. I love you!

Exercise
Love: How can you make room for God's love in your life every day?

_____

_____

_____Set a system, create a habit, I love to seek God first thing in the morning by reading scripture.

Body: Set a standard of how you will honor God in your body. Set guidelines for yourself. (Personally I declared I would no longer have sex before marriage and I would take care of my body to the best ability that I can by keeping it hydrated, fit, and feeding it healthy foods)

Memorize and meditate:
But without faith it is impossible to please and be satisfactory to him. For whoever would come near to God must believe that God exists and that He is the rewarder of those who earnestly and diligently seek him out.
Hebrews 11:6

DAY 31

Choose the narrow path

Enter through the narrow gate; for wide is the gate and spacious is the way that leads away to destruction, and many are those who are entering through it. But the gate is narrow and the way is straightened and compressed that leads away to life, and few are those who find it.
Matthew 7:13-14

"The way to victory is a narrow path that requires discipline regardless of our feelings. Follow faith, not feelings."
Joyce Meyer

Exercise
Love: How can I follow my faith and not my feelings today?

_____

_____

_____

Body: How can I better discipline my body despite of my feelings?

_____

_____

_____

Memorize and meditate:
This is my commandment that ye love one another as I have loved you.
John 15:12

Because if you acknowledge and confess with your lips that Jesus is Lord and in your heart believe (adhere to, trust in, and rely on the truth) that God raised Him from the dead, you will be saved. For with the heart a person believes (adheres to, trusts in, and relies on Christ) and so is justified (declared righteous, acceptable to God), and with the mouth he confesses (declares openly and speaks out freely his faith) and confirms {his} salvation. The scripture says, No man who believes in Him (who adheres to, relies on, and trusts in Him) will {ever} be put to shame or be disappointed.
Romans 10: 9-11

Our lives in our physical body will end at some point and time. What happens to our soul is based on our heart condition. God promises that those that have lived with a kind and loving heart, and have believed in Him, that believed that he sent Jesus to die for our sins will live an eternal life of peace.

I have lived without God in my life for a long time, and even though there were moments of joy much of that time was filled with confusion, anxiety, and stress. Since making God the center of my life, (at 29 years old) I have experienced PEACE. Joy that is inside me no matter what is going on in my life. Obstacles and hardships still exist, however there is an inner peace inside of me that cannot be moved. Through studying the Bible I am learning every day. I encourage you to believe that this feeling of peace is available to you as well. And it is through believing in God and Jesus Christ. I encourage you to study the Bible on your own, do your own research and decide that you want Jesus in your life for yourself. If you would like to say a simple prayer to allow God to be the center of your life and accept Jesus as your Lord and savior here is a prayer below. God bless you!

With Love,
Danielle

Father God, I love you. Jesus I believe in you. I believe that you died for my sins. I know that I am a sinner and I'm sorry for the way I've lived. I'm ready to turn away from sin and live a life with you. Thank you for forgiving me! Thank you for loving me! Please come into my heart right now and help me be the person you want me to be. Amen.

To contact the author, write to Danielle Swaby:
Swaby@Swabyway.com
Swabyway.com

I'd love to hear from you!

Made in the USA
San Bernardino, CA
18 June 2018